NEW YORK 2013

THE CITY AT A GLANCE

Manhattan Municipal Building

Adolph Alexander Weinman's golden stat...
Civic Fame tops McKim, Mead...
1914 Beaux Arts government...
It was the first building in New...
to incorporate a subway statio...
1 Centre Street

Brooklyn Bridge

Fly into JFK Airport and no doubt this is how
you'll cross the East River to arrive downtown.
It was designed by John Augustus Roebling,
who died before its completion in 1883.

Empire State Building

Architect William Lamb's skyscraper (King
Kong's favourite New York high-rise) opened
to the public in 1931. The views from the
86th floor observatory really are fabulous.
350 Fifth Avenue, T 212 736 3100

Chrysler Building

The ornamentation on this 1930 art deco gem,
designed by William Van Alen, was inspired
by the radiators and hubcaps of Chrysler cars.
405 Lexington Avenue

United Nations

This outstanding International Style complex,
with the Secretariat tower as its centrepiece, is
based on the designs of 11 architects. A massive
renovation project, which will run up a bill of
about $2bn, is scheduled to finish in 2014.
405 E 42nd Street

Manhattan Bridge

Connecting Manhattan and Brooklyn, Ralph
Modjeski and Leon Moisseiff's bridge, opened
in 1909, now carries seven lanes of traffic and
four subway tracks. An $834m reconstruction,
focused on improving safety and reducing
congestion, is due for completion by 2014.

INTRODUCTION
THE CHANGING FACE OF THE URBAN SCENE

Is New York back on its feet again? Definitely. There is little doubt that this urban Goliath was hit hard by the recession, but the city is in recovery mode. Real estate is selling, the dining scene is at full throttle, and fashionistas are snapping up their <u>Alexander Wang</u> (see p086). The Big Apple is back in action, even if the stealth wealth of a decade ago has been replaced by a less brash spending style. New Yorkers have developed an appreciation for originality and authenticity. Shops selling handmade or speciality goods, and restaurants presenting farm-to-table, market-driven menus tap into the desire for top-quality products with an innate sense of place. The glamour and the glitz are there, only now locals are demanding more for their buck – and from themselves.

Manhattan's West Side received a major injection of energy with André Balazs' hotel, <u>The Standard</u> (see p023), and the <u>High Line</u> (see p034), which should unveil its last stretch of walkway in 2014. And the development in this area is ongoing, with the ambitious Hudson Yards Project (see p064) underway. Elsewhere, artists and hipsters are still migrating to Brooklyn, especially to the brownstones of Bed-Stuy and Prospect Heights. A modern Harlem renaissance is also in full swing. Eateries are opening and townhouses are being renovated, and professionals (pushed out of their more conventional territories) are calling them home. Formerly on the fringes, these areas are the new epicentres of cool.

ESSENTIAL INFO

FACTS, FIGURES AND USEFUL ADDRESSES

TOURIST OFFICE
810 Seventh Avenue
T 212 484 1222
www.nycgo.com

TRANSPORT
Car hire
Avis
T 212 593 8378
www.avis.com
Hertz
T 212 486 5915
www.hertz.com
Car service
Carmel Car and Limousine Service
T 1 866 666 6666
Dial 7 Car & Limousine Service
T 212 777 7777
Subway
T 718 330 1234
www.mta.info
Trains run 24 hours a day, every day
Yellow cabs
T 212 639 9675 (for enquiries such as
lost property)

EMERGENCY SERVICES
Emergencies
T 911
Police (non-emergency)
T 311
24-hour pharmacy
CVS
630 Lexington Avenue
T 917 369 8688
www.cvs.com

CONSULATES
British Consulate
845 Third Avenue
T 212 745 0200
www.ukinusa.fco.gov.uk

POSTAL SERVICES
Post office
909 Third Avenue
T 1 800 275 8777
Shipping
UPS
T 212 680 3118
www.ups.com

BOOKS
**Block by Block: Jane Jacobs and the
Future of New York** edited by Timothy
Mennel, Jo Steffens and Christopher
Klemek (Princeton Architectural Press)
Here is New York by EB White
(Little Bookroom)

WEBSITES
Architecture/Design
www.cooperhewitt.org
Newspaper
www.nytimes.com

EVENTS
Frieze Art Fair
www.friezenewyork.com
ICFF
www.icff.com
New York Design Week
designweeknyc.org

COST OF LIVING
Taxi from JFK Airport to Manhattan
$55-60
Cappuccino
$3.50
Packet of cigarettes
$12
Daily newspaper
$2.50
Bottle of champagne
$65

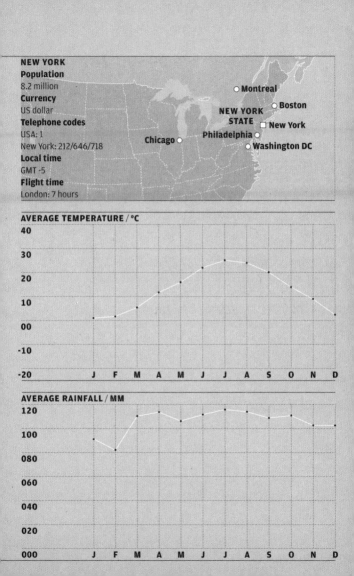

NEW YORK
Population
8.2 million
Currency
US dollar
Telephone codes
USA: 1
New York: 212/646/718
Local time
GMT -5
Flight time
London: 7 hours

Montreal

NEW YORK STATE
Boston
New York
Philadelphia
Washington DC
Chicago

AVERAGE TEMPERATURE / °C

| | J | F | M | A | M | J | J | A | S | O | N | D |
40
30
20
10
00
-10
-20

AVERAGE RAINFALL / MM

120
100
080
060
040
020
000

| J | F | M | A | M | J | J | A | S | O | N | D |

NEIGHBOURHOODS

THE AREAS YOU NEED TO KNOW AND WHY

To help you navigate the city, we've chosen the most interesting districts (see below and the map inside the back cover) and colour-coded our featured venues, according to their location; those venues that are outside these areas are not coloured.

TRIBECA/THE BATTERY

Manhattan's southern end could not be more diverse. Downtown's most compelling area, Ground Zero (see p009), remains in flux, still taking shape more than a decade after 9/11. Hip Tribeca is a younger version of Soho, with sophisticated restaurants such as Brushstroke (see p038).

UPPER WEST SIDE

Archetypal liberal intellectual territory, this residential area benefits from both old and new money. The vast Central Park West apartment blocks are like ocean liners steaming through Manhattan. Its cultural focal point is Lincoln Center (see p068), which was recently renovated.

WEST VILLAGE

Darling of both indie and global brands (especially along Bleecker Street), the leafy West Village has a vibrant yet intimate ambience. Here, Manhattan assumes a human scale, with cosy neighbourhood eateries, 19th-century townhouses and pretty streets, such as Perry and Charles.

SOHO

Once an artists' quarter, where cast-iron buildings were transformed into post-industrial lofts and studios, the vibe is now more Kenzo than De Kooning, and Soho can feel like a tourist trap. However, it does have cool stores such as Kiosk (see p077), good galleries and boutique hotels, including The James (see p027).

UPPER EAST SIDE

This is quintessential rich-bitch New York, replete with liveried doormen helping social X-rays carry bag upon bag after a hard day's shopping on Madison Avenue. The area is also where you'll find the city's most important museums. For lunch, try The Wright (see p055) at the Guggenheim.

MIDTOWN

Manhattan's central business district is the home of Times Square – the backdrop for the bright lights of Broadway or a tacky, neon-lit, tourist hell, depending on your take. It also has one of New York's highest concentrations of hotels. Highlights include the Museum of Arts and Design (see p036).

CHELSEA

The unmissable attraction here is the High Line (see p034); the area is also an epicentre for art (see p035). Modish venues such as Hôtel Americano (see p017) and its rooftop bar/lounge, La Piscine (see p052), have helped to restore a cool factor that gentrification had diminished.

EAST VILLAGE/LOWER EAST SIDE

Traditionally a working-class, immigrant area, the Lower East Side is still a cultural melting pot, and home to some of NYC's edgier galleries, bars and clubs, as well as SANAA's New Museum (see p071). To the north, the East Village has been heading upmarket since the 1980s, while Noho draws fashionistas to its trendy boutiques.

LANDMARKS

THE SHAPE OF THE CITY SKYLINE

How can you pick out a landmark building in a city that possibly contains more instantly recognisable skyscrapers than any other? Perhaps owing to its relative youth, New York has never been shy about making a statement with its modern architecture. And thanks to the wealth of many of its citizens, the Big Apple has been able to call on the talents of almost every architect of note of the past 100 or so years, to help create its incomparable skyline.

Many recent developments in the metropolis have been slowed by the recession, and in the case of the World Trade Center site by political wrangling – the configuring of such an emotive location was never going to be straightforward. The overall plan comprises five main towers, with the National September 11 Memorial & Museum (Albany Street/Greenwich Street, T 212 266 5211) at the heart of the complex. Michael Arad and Peter Walker and Partners' dramatic plaza, and the subterranean museum, by Davis Brody Bond, entered via Snøhetta's pavilion, are now open. Rearing above them, and due to complete by the end of 2013, are the first two towers to have topped out: the 541m One World Trade Center (West Street/Vesey Street), by SOM's David Childs, which will be the third-tallest building in the world; and the less attention-grabbing but quietly impressive 298m Four World Trade Center (150 Greenwich Street), designed by Fumihiko Maki.
For full addresses, see Resources.

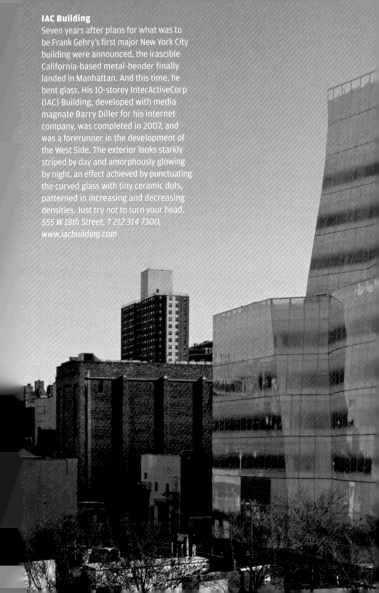

IAC Building

Seven years after plans for what was to be Frank Gehry's first major New York City building were announced, the irascible California-based metal-bender finally landed in Manhattan. And this time, he bent glass. His 10-storey InterActiveCorp (IAC) Building, developed with media magnate Barry Diller for his internet company, was completed in 2007, and was a forerunner in the development of the West Side. The exterior looks starkly striped by day and amorphously glowing by night, an effect achieved by punctuating the curved glass with tiny ceramic dots, patterned in increasing and decreasing densities. Just try *not* to turn your head.
555 W 18th Street, T 212 314 7300,
www.iacbuilding.com

AT&T Building

This massive 1932 art deco structure, designed by American architect Ralph Walker, was known originally as the AT&T Long Distance Building; it housed the telecommunications giant's transatlantic offices and equipment. In the 1990s, the company made this its HQ, although AT&T has since sold up. Its brick-clad bulk (all 105,500 sq m of it) is quintessentially Gotham-like in form, with the lobby boasting the obligatory tiled map of the world on one wall. The building may not be one of the city's best-known landmarks, nor even Walker's best work (this is usually said to be the former Irving Trust Company headquarters at 1 Wall Street). However, from its profile to the materials used, the AT&T could not be found anywhere except New York, and for that it is a masterwork.
32 Sixth Avenue

Hearst Tower

Fresh from his remodelling of the London skyline with 30 St Mary Axe, Norman Foster tackled the HQ of the Hearst media empire. The diamond-faceted facade of this 46-storey tower, completed in 2006, thrusts out of an existing art deco building that was commissioned in the 1920s by media mogul William Randolph Hearst; the six-storey structure was always intended to form the base of a landmark tower. The new blends seamlessly with the old, thanks to the dramatic lobby that rises up through the lower floors to provide access to all parts of the building. And it's not just a pretty sight. The tower is environmentally sensitive too – it was constructed with more than 85 per cent recycled steel and consumes about a quarter less energy than its neighbours. *300 W 57th Street, www.hearst.com*

Austrian Cultural Forum

In a city where big is often thought to be better, Austrian architect Raimund Abraham created a small wonder in 2002 with his first major US project, although he had lived in New York for more than 30 years. 'My intention with the building was to resolve the extreme condition of smallness of the site,' he said. Abraham, who died in 2010, succeeded. The Cultural Forum is a brilliant design: a glass-skinned sliver, a mere 7.6m wide, rising 85m. The building's presence belies its dimensions. It also outshines its neighbours with its brooding facade, which is reminiscent, in profile, of an Easter Island statue. When it was unveiled, it was hailed by many as the most important structure to have been built in Manhattan in 40 years.
11 E 52nd Street, T 212 319 5300,
www.acfny.org

Woolworth Building

For some 17 years after its opening in 1913, Cass Gilbert's Woolworth Building was the tallest in the world. His client, five-and-dime-store magnate Frank W Woolworth, was wealthy enough to pay the $13.5m price tag in cash. This, coupled with Gilbert's soaring gothic proportions, earned it the moniker 'the cathedral of commerce'. Even today, the scale of the building is impressive: it stands 241.4m high, and there's room for 14,000 workers on 54 floors of office space, all of which are served by 30 elevators. The only area open to the public is the dazzling marble-clad lobby, which is lined with medieval-style gargoyles, including a caricature of Woolworth counting his money, and Gilbert, like Justinian with his Hagia Sophia, cradling his monument.

233 Broadway

HOTELS

WHERE TO STAY AND WHICH ROOMS TO BOOK

There's buoyancy in the Big Apple's hotel scene, with launches all across town. Over on the West Side, Hôtel Americano (opposite) is Grupo Habita's contribution to this area's bold developments, and brings with it a buzzy social scene. Different in style, but just as seductive, is The NoMad (see po20), which also has a sexy bar and restaurant. Developed by the Sydell Group's Andrew Zobler, it's a block away from the ever-fashionable Ace (see po28), also a Sydell project, in the area dubbed North of Madison Square Park.

Among the dizzying array of hotels in Midtown, our picks are The Chatwal (see po21), whose deco-themed rooms are the ideal retreat from the lively in-house Lambs Club restaurant (T 212 997 5262); and, for a blow-out, the Four Seasons (see po31). On the Upper East Side, The Surrey (20 E 76th Street, T 212 288 3700) is an art-lined luxury hideaway, or consider the discreet charms of The Lowell (28 E 63rd Street, T 212 838 1400).

Hipsters should make their base in Williamsburg at the Wythe Hotel (see po18), or on Manhattan's Lower East Side at The Nolitan (see po26) or the Thompson LES (190 Allen Street, T 212 460 5300). The Thompson's upscale take on Japanese pub food at Blue Ribbon Sushi Izakaya (T 212 466 0404) is not to be missed. If you're in the city on business, check into the Andaz Wall Street (see po30), the slickest reservation in the financial district.

For full addresses and room rates, see Resources.

Hôtel Americano

Tucked inside Chelsea's gallery district (see p035), Grupo Habita's first American hotel is a class act, from architect Enrique Norten's mesh-covered building to the sleek interiors by Parisian designer Arnaud Montigny. The 56 rooms exude urban cool, with low platform beds and contemporary furnishings in a palette of black, grey and yellow; the ninth-floor Uptown Studio (above) is among the best.

The rooftop lounge, La Piscine (see p052), serves up crisp cocktails and knockout views of the High Line (see p034), while downstairs, in The Americano restaurant (T 212 525 0000), chef Joseph Buenconsejo creates zippy French cuisine with Latin touches. The vibe is laidback but full of brio, especially during Sunday brunch. *518 W 27th Street, T 212 216 0000, www.hotel-americano.com*

Wythe Hotel
Opened in 2012, the Wythe has given
Brooklyn the grown-up hotel it deserves.
The factory building has been wisely
preserved, and the decor of reclaimed
pine furniture and bespoke wallpaper
(King Room, pictured) is the right foil,
softening the industrial edge. Dine at
Reynard (T 718 460 8004), then drink
in the Manhattan skyline from the bar.
80 Wythe Avenue, T 718 460 8000

The NoMad Hotel

Injecting a shot of lavishness into Midtown, The NoMad marries old-world charm with New York sophistication in a turn-of-the-century Beaux Arts building. Attention to historical detail characterises Jacques Garcia's treatment of the 168 rooms and public areas, such as the lobby (above). Vintage Heriz rugs cover a salvaged maple floor and the library's 200-year-old spiral staircase was imported from France.

Reserve a lofty Grande Room on the second or third floor, or a Suite for a diverting street vista. The restaurant, NoMad (T 347 472 5660), is run by Will Guidara and Daniel Humm of Michelin-starred Eleven Madison Park (T 212 889 0905). Maison Kitsuné opened its first American boutique on the ground floor. *1170 Broadway, T 212 796 1500, www.thenomadhotel.com*

The Chatwal

This 1905 building was originally designed by architect Stanford White. In 2010, it was overhauled by Thierry Despont, who applied his own updated version of art deco in dazzling fashion. The 76 guest rooms, including the grand Producer Suite (above), are decorated with vintage 'steamer trunk' wardrobes, fine suede walls and old subway signs. Off the lobby, in The Lambs Club restaurant (see p016),

Geoffrey Zakarian collects rave reviews for his modern American cuisine. The 18th-century French stone fireplace, red-leather banquettes and warm lighting make a handsome backdrop for the equally alluring food, which pairs like a charm with the cocktails whipped up by NYC nightlife veteran Sasha Petraske. *130 W 44th Street, T 212 764 6200, www.thechatwalny.com*

Crosby Street Hotel

Although it's right in the heart of the city, Crosby Street is one of those New York thoroughfares that feels off-the-radar. Rising 11 storeys above a former parking lot, the red-brick Crosby Street Hotel (the only American outpost for Britain's Firmdale Hotel group) feels old New York outside, new New York inside. In the lobby, which has full-height windows, Kit Kemp introduced colourful paintings and fabrics, and a monumental metal skull sculpture by Jaume Plensa. Vintage dressmaker's mannequins and oversized headboards set a quirky tone in the 86 rooms, which overlook Soho; opt for a One Bedroom Suite (above). Belly up to The Crosby Bar, decorated in a cheery style, for well-crafted cocktails and small plates. *79 Crosby Street, T 212 226 6400, www.firmdale.com*

The Standard High Line

Like his classic Soho hotel, The Mercer (T 212 966 6060), André Balazs' Standard took a long time to see the light of day. The 337-room tower finally opened in 2009, and, a few years on, it has become something of a landmark. Looming 18m over the High Line (see p034), the hulking slab of glass, perched on concrete pylons, juts into the West Side skyline. Beyond the lobby (above), the rooms are compact, but benefit from this area's low-slung warehouses, giving unobstructed city or Hudson River views. Designers Roman and Williams added elements such as wood tambour panelling, which extends up the rooms' walls and across the ceiling. The Standard Grill (T 212 645 4100) and Living Room bar still pull in a lively crowd. *848 Washington Street, T 212 645 4646, www.standardhotels.com*

Gramercy Park Hotel
Ian Schrager and Julian Schnabel's transformation of the Gramercy Park was an instant hit when it was unveiled in 2006. And it still rocks. The opulent common areas, including the Drawing Room (pictured), drip with art by the likes of Damien Hirst and Andy Warhol. The reopened Gramercy Terrace on the roof dishes up classic American cuisine.
2 Lexington Avenue, T 212 920 3300

The Nolitan

Design firm Grzywinski+Pons were faced with the challenge of creating a sense of community within a community for the Nolita area's first boutique hotel. The result is an industrial-chic low-rise that blends in well with its surroundings. Inside are 55 snug rooms, with oak flooring, concrete ceilings, Corian accents and floor-to-ceiling windows; some have private balconies. The public areas are generous – there's a spacious roof terrace and an open-plan ground floor connecting the lobby (above) with a library and a café. The Nolitan's amenities (including bicycles) are comprehensive enough to attract both business travellers and trendsetters, and despite residing on a traffic-heavy street corner, the hotel maintains a serene aura. *30 Kenmare Street, T 212 925 2555, www.nolitanhotel.com*

The James

Designed by Eran Chen of architects ODA, The James has a boxy, almost brutalist facade and appears to float on stilts cantilevered above elegant terraced gardens. Inside, the aesthetic is just as daring, courtesy of in-house curator Matthew Jensen. Working with Artists Space, he has devoted each of the 14 floors to artists such as Aaron Wexler and Sun K Kwak. As for the rooms, dark wooden headboards rise above white beds, and there are rainshowers hidden by translucent screens. Accommodations are on the small side, although massive windows let in plenty of light. Unwind by the rooftop pool (above), dropping down to the subterranean David Burke Kitchen (T 212 201 9119) for a bite to eat. *27 Grand Street, T 212 465 2000, www.jameshotel.com*

Ace Hotel
In 2009, the first East Coast offshoot of this Seattle-based chain signalled the start of more design-savvy times for the Nomad area. Playing on the Americana theme, with vintage and custom-made furnishings, New York City's Roman and Williams created a look that still feels cool. Check into Loft 811 (pictured) and chill in Rudy's Barbershop (see p090).
20 W 29th Street, T 212 679 2222

Andaz Wall Street

Wall Street seems like a logical location for a full-service, luxury hotel, but previous efforts have either fallen short or failed outright. The Andaz, designed by David Rockwell, is Hyatt's attempt, making the most of a prime position and learning from its predecessors' missteps. Housed in a former Barclays Bank building, built in 1982, the hotel's standard lobby and check-in desk have been replaced by a lounge with an iPad-wielding host. The 253 rooms are large and well proportioned. We plumped for Room 1513 (above); those facing south-west look on to Hanover Square. The cuisine in Wall & Water (T 212 699 1700), the Andaz's mod-American restaurant, is so tasty you'll be happy the lower-level gym is open 24 hours. *75 Wall Street, T 212 590 1234, www.andaz.com*

Four Seasons

It's the Four Seasons, so of course it's faultless. Perhaps the Canadian group's crown jewel, the IM Pei-designed tower is still said to be the city's tallest hotel, and by golly does the Chinese-born architect give good power lobby. The service is exemplary, and as for the rooms, they may not all be to our taste but they are large and luxurious; the 400 sq m Ty Warner Penthouse (above), is stunning (and pricey, being the world's third-most expensive hotel suite). At a pinch, we think the views looking north over Central Park are the best, but the southern aspect is pretty good too. Cap off your day in an oversized chair by the fireplace in the Ty Lounge with a flawless martini and some gripping people-watching.
57 E 57th Street, T 212 758 5700, www.fourseasons.com/newyork

24 HOURS

SEE THE BEST OF THE CITY IN JUST ONE DAY

Manhattan offers some of the best walking in the world. Head in any direction and you can be sure of seeing something interesting within the first few blocks. The problem is not how to fill a day, but how to fit so much in. Luckily, you'll visit this city more than once, so you can concentrate on the must-sees one trip at a time. For example, MoMA in Midtown (11 W 53rd Street, T 212 708 9400) and the Museum Mile running up the east side of Central Park, including the Whitney (945 Madison Avenue, T 212 570 3600), The Met (1000 Fifth Avenue, T 212 535 7710), Guggenheim (1071 Fifth Avenue, T 212 423 3500) and Cooper-Hewitt (2 E 91st Street, T 212 849 8400), is a weekend's worth of culture alone. Then there are the shops (see p072): to come to NYC and not drop a coin would be like going to Amsterdam and not crossing a canal. And let's not forget the neighbouring borough of Brooklyn. Minutes away from Manhattan across the East River and brimming with terrific restaurants and boutiques, Williamsburg, easily accessible on the subway (take the L train), is a great place to kick off.

Rather than attempt the impossible, the 24 hours suggested here is a snapshot of New York through the eyes of a local, with glimpses of a handful of the exciting places that make up this miraculous metropolis. Not everything will be to everyone's taste, of course, but how will you know until you've tried?

For full addresses, see Resources.

11.00 Roebling Tea Room

For a first take on Williamsburg's diverse and booming scene, linger over a late breakfast in this former industrial space, frequented by restaurant folk, musicians and artists. Conceived by owner Syd Silver, the airy, high-ceilinged interior, with its green-tiled bar, oozes easy-going charm. Chef Dennis Spina does comfort food with a twist. Vegetarians will be gratified by the signature breakfast of warm beets and poached eggs with goat's cheese over kale; and the house burger – a huge grass-fed patty, slathered in a secret sauce – should sate meat-eaters. Pair with a mug of Crop to Cup coffee. Afterwards, check out the art at nearby Parker's Box Gallery (T 718 388 2882). For a top-up cup to go, visit Toby's Estate Coffee (T 347 457 6160). *143 Roebling Street, T 718 963 0760, www.roeblingtearoom.com*

14.00 High Line

A green strip of elevated parkway in West Manhattan has been the regeneration project on everyone's lips for the past few years. This abandoned 1930s rail track was threatened with demolition in the late 1990s, so two local residents, Robert Hammond and Joshua David, stepped in to form a non-profit group, Friends of the High Line, to save it. The result, designed by architects Diller Scofidio + Renfro, and James Corner Field Operations, is an inspired public space, used from dawn to dusk. The first section, from Gansevoort Street to 20th Street, opened in 2009, and a second section, extending to 30th Street, was finished in 2011. Its final phase, The High Line at the Rail Yards, is due to open in 2014 and will stretch uptown, wrapping around Hudson Yards (see p064).
T 212 206 9922, www.thehighline.org

15.00 Chelsea galleries

Exit the High Line at W 20th Street and you'll drop into West Chelsea. Following the start of the area's regeneration, the focus has been on this once-sleepy part of town. Hôtel Americano (see p017) drew more attention to the locality, and Tenth Avenue now bustles with great restaurants, such as Cookshop (T 212 924 4440). This is also the gallery district. New Yorkers take their art seriously – even more so since the launch of NYCs own Frieze Art Fair in 2012 – and like modern-day Medicis, they don't just buy pieces, they are collectors. Stroll along Tenth Avenue to see this week's wunderkinds. Call into the Gagosian at 555 W 24th Street (above; T 212 741 1111), which also has a gallery on W 21st Street (T 212 741 1717); Mary Boone on W 24th Street (T 212 752 2929); and David Zwirner on W 19th Street (T 212 517 8677).

17.00 MAD

Formerly the American Craft Museum on W 53rd Street, MAD (Museum of Arts and Design) opened here, on Columbus Circle, in 2008. An update of an existing 1964 Edward Durell Stone building (which New Yorkers famously loved to hate), the museum's new home was designed by Brad Cloepfil of the Portland-based Allied Works Architecture. Derided by some as far too radical a reworking of Stone's original modernist design, Cloepfil's building is dramatic from the outside in, the facade a bold, interlocking pattern of glass and glazed terracotta panels. The museum's interior comprises 1,300 sq m of space, showing exhibitions of modern American and international design. Closed Mondays.
2 Columbus Circle, T 212 299 7777, www.madmuseum.org

20.00 Brushstroke

For his latest venture, housed in an 1860s brick building in Tribeca, famed New York chef/restaurateur David Bouley teamed up with Osaka's Tsuji Culinary Institute. The house speciality is kaiseki: a multi-course, seasonal, traditional Japanese meal that requires years of training to master. To keep the chefs' preparations as the focal point, Tokyo-based design firm Super Potato devised an airy, clean-lined dining room, choosing warm blondwood for the walls, floors, tables and chairs. An L-shaped bar cradles the open kitchen to maintain transparency between cooks and diners. Windows, on the other hand, are lined with rice paper to filter bright light and ensure privacy. Bouley recently added a sushi bar, helmed by Eiji Ichimura. *30 Hudson Street, T 212 791 3771, www.davidbouley.com*

23.00 Experimental Cocktail Club

It was only a matter of time before Romée de Goriainoff, Pierre-Charles Cros and Olivier Bon's American-cocktail-inspired phenomenon arrived stateside. And like its Paris and London sisters, the New York outpost offers premium spirits and has a facade so discreet it's almost undetectable. Once you're in, the fun begins. Dorothée Meilichzon decked out the two-room den with a pressed-tin ceiling, low-dangling lights, armchairs and a marble fireplace, creating a space that drips with style, yet has a relaxed air. Mixologist Nicolas de Soto has devised a menu of 14 complex libations, but is happy to create something bespoke. To visit, send a reservation request via e-mail. Party on at cabaret spot The Box (T 212 982 9301), next door. *191 Chrystie Street,*
www.experimentalcocktailclubny.com

URBAN LIFE
CAFÉS, RESTAURANTS, BARS AND NIGHTCLUBS

The city's recently opened venues reflect an optimistic, inventi
mood. Small plates continue to reign, with the elaborate tasti
menu at Atera (77 Worth Street, T 212 226 1444) topping our l
For a moderate bill, try Japanese pub Family Recipe (231 Eldri
Street, T 212 529 3133), the dim sum at RedFarm (529 Huds
Street, T 212 792 9700), or the new-American spot Recette (3
W 12th Street, T 212 414 3000). The star chefs are shaking up th
formulas, with Daniel Boulud pushing his upmarket menu i
Mediterranean direction at Boulud Sud (20 W 64th Street, T 212 5
1313) and Marc Forgione pulling the crowds at his eponymo
urban-rustic Tribeca restaurant (134 Reade Street, T 212 941 94(
Kutsher's Tribeca (186 Franklin Street, T 212 431 0606) serv
Jewish-American cuisine in a sleek interior by Rafael de Cárder

The hip-hotel scene shows no sign of slowing (see p016). Ha
rooftop or poolside drinks at La Piscine (see p052), Jimmy
The James (see p027), The Beach at Dream Downtown (355
16th Street, T 212 229 2336) or Haven at the Sanctuary Hotel (.
W 47th Street, T 212 466 9000). A trip out to Brooklyn will rewa
you with standout restaurants such as Potlikker (338 Bedf(
Avenue, T 718 388 9808) and Colonie (127 Atlantic Avenue, T :
855 7500). After hours, hang out at Donna (see p042) or, back
Manhattan, at Acme (9 Great Jones Street, T 212 203 2121).
For full addresses, see Resources.

Miss Lily's

This spirited Caribbean joint, designed by New York nightlife impresario Serge Becker (Joe's Pub, La Esquina, The Box), is a whole lot of fun. The front dining room is tiny – just 20 tables and an abbreviated bar – but the city's stylish set congregate in the dimly lit, loungey back room. The decor, inspired by Brooklyn's traditional Jamaican chicken joints, is a mishmash of chequerboard floors, laminate booths and album-covered walls. There's a pulsing ska and reggae soundtrack, and the gorgeous staff sizzle as much as the dishes that they serve: fiery jerk chicken, and cod fritters. Pop next door to Miss Lily's Bake Shop (T 646 588 5375), a record shop/café incorporating Melvin's Juice Box, helmed by local juicing legend Melvin Major Jr. *132 W Houston Street, T 646 588 5375, www.misslilysnyc.com*

Donna

Despite its location in a quieter corner of south Williamsburg, Donna has become a destination for cocktail and design devotees. Aiming for a laidback, Central American atmosphere, owner Leif Huckman partnered with the Haslegrave brothers from Brooklyn-based design firm hOmE to create the art deco-inspired interior, in a mid-1800s building. The dramatic, white vaulted ceiling, delicate steel light fixtures (a Haslegrave speciality), hand-tiled bar stools and salvaged pine flooring from Tall Cotton Supply all channel a Spanish colonial mood. Bar manager Jeremy Oertel's cocktails pay homage to Huckman's Honduran roots. Pair the tequila-based Smokey Peach or menthol amaro-infused Brancolad with small, deftly prepared plates, such as oxtail relish-filled avocados and chorizo empanadas.
27 Broadway, www.donnabklyn.com

James

The brownstone-lined Prospect Heights is Brooklyn at its classic best, with none of nearby Williamsburg's arty grunge or Bed-Stuy's grit. It's a natural location for James, the refined restaurant named after the great-grandfather of chef Bryan Calvert, who co-founded the venue with his wife, Deborah Williamson. The couple designed the interior themselves, restoring the original pressed-tin ceiling and white brick walls, and accenting the dining area with plants and a Lucite chandelier. The food is new American, and many of the greens are freshly picked from the adjacent herb garden. The pressed chicken and Berkshire Pork Belly confit are exceptional. To enjoy a less expensive meal, drop by on Monday for burger night or for Sunday supper. *605 Carlton Avenue, T 718 942 4255, www.jamesrestaurantny.com*

Scarpetta

Scott Conant redefined Italian cooking in New York with his Midtown restaurants Alto and L'Impero. Both were highly esteemed, but Conant scored even better in the Meatpacking District with Scarpetta, set in a former townhouse. The dining room's pared-back cream-and-brown decor keeps the focus on the superbly executed food, although the retractable sunroof offset by timber beams is one flashy touch. The pastas are perfect: the ravioli, and the spaghetti with tomato and basil are reminders of how gratifying simple food can be. Conant's skill with less ubiquitous meats such as rabbit, which he braises and tucks into pasta, is another lure. The wine list is fairly priced and is anchored around Italy and France.
355 W 14th Street, T 212 691 0555, www.scarpettanyc.com

DBGB Kitchen & Bar

In 2008, Daniel Boulud led the Upper
West Side's French-cuisine revival with
Bar Boulud (T 212 595 0303), not far
from Lincoln Center (see p068). This
was followed by DBGB downtown. A
riff on legendary nightclub CBGB, it's
a reasonably priced bistro inspired
by the nearby kitchen-supply shops,
serving a meat-focused menu.
299 Bowery, T 212 933 5300

Red Rooster

Whatever the time of day, there's always a buzz at Marcus Samuelsson's restaurant, situated in the epicentre of Harlem. The Ethiopian-born, Swedish-raised chef's upbeat personality is reflected in the snazzy interior, which is lined with art by Sanford Biggers, Ming Smith and Philip Maysles. Usually packed and humming, the venue attracts a diverse crowd, whether it's to the dining room (opposite), grocery (above) or the bar. The global menu is unique; try some crispy yard bird (fried chicken), Helga's meatballs, or dirty rice and shrimp. Sunday brunch is a raucous, no-reservations affair, when a gospel singer weaves amid diners. Downstairs, Ginny's Supper Club (T 212 421 3821) offers a blend of live music, cocktails and food. *310 Lenox Avenue, T 212 792 9001, www.redroosterharlem.com*

Tertulia

Inspired by the *sidrerias* (cider houses) of Asturias in northern Spain, Tertulia (well praised by the critics) marries conviviality with tapas-style cuisine. To create a Spanish-inflected space in this former Prohibition-era speakeasy, chef Seamus Mullen, formerly of Boqueria, partnered with designer Jason Volenec. The ceiling arches, oak tables, barnyard door, and wood-burning stove at the front of the open kitchen all set a rustic tone. Mullen's food reinforces the authentic Spanish theme through more familiar dishes such as the *jamón serrano* and *croquetas*, as well as comprising original creations – Cojonudo Revisited is two bites of rich and savoury creamy quail's egg and smoky pig's cheek.
359 Sixth Avenue, T 646 559 9909, www.tertulianyc.com

Co

Launched in 2009 by local bread-making supremo Jim Lahey, founder of Sullivan St Bakery, this Chelsea pizzeria delivers some of the best pies in town. Pull up to one of its (no-reservation) communal tables and take your time choosing from the menu. Each pizza has a compelling name, such as The Flambé, a mound of parmesan and béchamel, with caramelised onions, thick lardons and mozzarella.

Lahey studied sculpture before he hotfooted it to Italy, to learn how to bake bread in small batches – a craft he has perfected. The main Sullivan St Bakery (T 212 265 5580) is in Hell's Kitchen, and Lahey recently opened an offshoot a few doors down from Co, selling sandwiches and its own granola as well as bread. *230 Ninth Avenue, T 212 243 1105, www.co-pane.com*

La Piscine

Mix a dose of Mexican hospitality with a dash of French seduction, and you get this impossibly cool pool lounge crowning Hôtel Americano (see p017). Named after the 1969 film starring Romy Schneider and Alain Delon, La Piscine radiates nonchalant glamour. The main area is furnished, for the most part, with Brazilian furniture from Espasso (see p072), and retractable glass walls mean the restaurant area can host diners all year. Joseph Buenconsejo's Greek-inspired summer menu is based on simple grilled seafood, meats and salads; winter dishes have an Alpine edge. The cocktail bar serves delicious libations and a long list of mescals. You don't have to enter the hotel to reach La Piscine — an exterior lift whisks you straight up. *Hôtel Americano, 518 W 27th Street, T 212 525 0000, www.hotel-americano.com*

Momofuku Ssäm Bar

Korean-American David Chang seemingly came out of nowhere to establish himself as one of New York's most exciting chefs. His cluster of restaurants includes the Midtown Má Pêche (T 212 757 5878) and a trio of East Village venues, including the flagship Momofuku Ssäm Bar. Injecting new vigour into the played-out pan-Asian genre, Chang's food celebrates the colours, flavours and textures of the orient, and presents some unexpected flourishes. Long, narrow and sleek, with stools and communal tables, MSB does not take reservations, but any queueing is worth the wait, we assure you. Try the signature steamed pork buns, which are stuffed with crisp pork strips, hoisin sauce, spring onions and pickled cucumber. *207 Second Avenue, T 212 254 3500, www.momofuku.com*

The Wright

As two of the most sensory experiences, fine art and fine dining would seem naturally complementary. The Wright restaurant at the Guggenheim Museum achieves an elegant balance between culture and cuisine. Named after the Guggenheim's architect, Frank Lloyd Wright, the ground-level dining room is defined by a single, site-specific work: a bright, dynamic sculpture by British New York-based artist Liam Gillick. Crafted from slender, colourful aluminium panels, it has a futuristic appeal. As for the food, Mexico City-born executive chef Rodolfo Contreras, whose training included a stint in David Bouley's restaurant group, draws on local produce wherever possible for his simple yet stylish dishes.
1071 Fifth Avenue, T 212 427 5690, www.thewrightrestaurant.com

Pulino's

Keith McNally, credited by many with
inventing the restaurant-as-destination
genre, has created this homage to the
traditional Italian pizzeria. Helmed by
chef Tony Liu, Pulino's specialises in thin-
crust pizza with classic toppings. There
are breakfast and brunch menus too,
like semolina waffles and lemon scones.
282 Bowery, T 212 226 1966,
www.pulinosny.com

Talde

Food trends come and go, but Dale Talde is on a mission to summon one, pan-Asian, back into favour. And the long queues and good reviews at his Park Slope restaurant prove that Talde (formerly of Manhattan's Morimoto and Buddakan) is doing a fine job of that. The characterful canteen has mahogany carvings from a Pennsylvanian antiques warehouse, and window frames and mantelpieces salvaged in New York from an early 20th-century mansion's 'oriental study'. The intricately carved dragons and samurai warriors are by Maeda Yasube Yoshitsugu, known for his work in Japanese shrines in the mid-19th century. The menu is a tasty Asian tour via dishes such as pretzel pork and chive dumplings, and crispy bacon pad thai. *369 7th Avenue, T 347 916 0031, www.taldebrooklyn.com*

Ardesia

Ardesia is a blueprint for a neighbourhood wine bar: an enticing space with a friendly atmosphere. Designed by the architect Mimi Madigan, the lofty interior features Venetian stone in the bars, custom-made sofas and David Chipperfield taps in the bathrooms. Located in Hell's Kitchen, the venue is owned by Mandy Oser, who honed her skills at venerable seafood restaurant Le Bernardin (T 212 554 1515).

The wine list runs to about 100 bottles, selected from both the new and old worlds, with some unexpected countries represented, such as Slovenia and Greece. Prices are fair, and there are plenty of options by the glass. Amorette Casaus cooks up the small plates, and there's a nice selection of artisanal cheeses. *510 W 52nd Street, T 212 247 9191, www.ardesia-ny.com*

Bemelmans Bar

Adjacent to the lobby of the 1930 Carlyle hotel, Bemelmans is a city institution, a charming reminder of old New York. The long granite bar, grand piano, leather banquette and 24-carat gold-leaf ceilings are all familiar, if slightly stodgy, design elements. Yet when juxtaposed with the whimsical murals of Ludwig Bemelmans, author and illustrator of *Madeline*, the children's book first published in 1939, the mood lightens as the appeal widens. The servers are jacketed and the ambience is sophisticated but never stifling; everyone is welcomed warmly. Locals appreciate the discreet ambience and Bemelmans' signature cocktails; order a Patron Starlet or a Passion Royale. Music aficionados adore the live piano performances.
35 E 76th Street, T 212 744 1600,
www.rosewoodhotels.com

INSIDER'S GUIDE

SIKI IM, FASHION DESIGNER

Born and raised in Cologne, Germany, architect-turned-menswear-designer Siki Im works in Soho. But after living in Manhattan for a decade, it's Cobble Hill in Brooklyn that he now calls home. 'My neighbourhood reminds me of how I grew up. I go to the cheese shop to get cheese, and the butcher for meat,' says Im.

He kicks off his day with a hit of Toby's Estate coffee from Van Leeuwen (81 Bergen Street, T 718 701 1630). After working in the studio, he'll head to Il Buco (47 Bond Street, T 212 533 1932) for an artisanal Italian dinner, or Do Hwa (55 Carmine Street, T 212 414 1224) for 'the only good downtown Korean food'. Closer to home, Im favours the refined Southern comforts at Seersucker (329 Smith Street, T 718 422 0444) and market-driven dishes at The Grocery (288 Smith Street, T 718 596 3335). Drinking is a low-key affair, with 'a Kölsch beer, a patio and a mellow vibe' at Lavender Lake (383 Carroll Street, T 347 799 2154) in Gowanus.

In his leisure time, Im offsets his intense work schedule by steering clear of Manhattan. In addition to hanging in Prospect Park – 'a chilled version of Central Park' – he enjoys perusing the wares at the Saturday Fort Greene Flea (176 Lafayette Avenue) and getting visual inspiration at the Brooklyn Museum (200 Eastern Parkway, T 718 638 5000). To escape the city completely, Im heads out to Long Island (see p102), 'where the surf is good'.

For full addresses, see Resources.

ARCHITOUR

A GUIDE TO NEW YORK'S ICONIC BUILDINGS

Chicago may be the birthplace of the skyscraper, Dubai may boast the world's tallest structure, and Shanghai may have more towers, but perhaps no city is as closely identified with the high-rise as New York. Money was the motivation to reach for the sky, but symbolism has always been immensely important here, from the automotive fantasies of the art deco Chrysler Building (405 Lexington Avenue) to the soaring form of One World Trade Center (see p009). Indeed, maybe Gothamites' inordinate love of towers has been the reason that New York has managed to retain such a vibrant city centre, whereas so many of its American sister conurbations have become prisoners of suburban sprawl.

Right now, eyes are on the West Side of Manhattan, above 28th Street, where the redevelopment of this once gritty zone hugging the river is progressing. Kohn Pedersen Fox is master planner of the Hudson Yards Project (www.hydc.org), which will encompass a subway extension to line 7, mixed-use complexes and green space. Meanwhile, the debate rages on about the future of the New York Library's landmark Beaux Arts building (42nd Street/Fifth Avenue, T 917 275 6975). No one disagrees that something must be done to turn round its fortunes – the question is what. Norman Foster has submitted plans to modernise the interior and convert it into a lending library, but the preservationists are in uproar. *For full addresses, see Resources.*

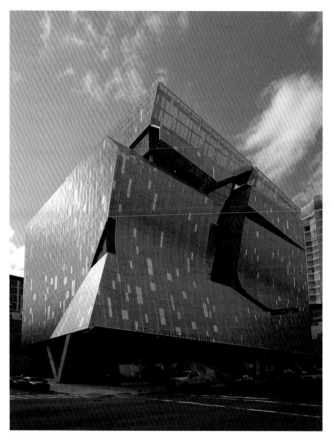

41 Cooper Square

Apart from the New Museum (see p071), it had been a while since this part of downtown had seen an important piece of new architecture. Which is why Cooper Union's 2009 School of Engineering and Faculty of Humanities and Social Sciences building was such a satisfying arrival. Home to one of America's most prominent higher-education institutions, the nine-storey structure was designed by Thom Mayne of Morphosis, in association with fellow Californian practice Gruzen Samton. A basic box shape has been distorted with jutting angles and a split facade draped in steel, creating a sense of fluidity and motion in spite of the hulking proportions. Inside the building, striking features include skywalks, a full-height atrium and a four-storey central staircase. *41 Cooper Square, www.cooper.edu*

Seagram Building

Mies van der Rohe's 1958 masterpiece typified his less-is-more philosophy and is a triumph of the International Style. In fact, he stated this was his only building in the US to meet his stringent European standards of design, borrowed from the architect's classic German Pavilion built for the 1929 Barcelona World's Fair. It was the first building to feature floor-to-ceiling windows, to achieve the modernist ideal of a curtain of glass, and although American construction codes prevented him from displaying the structural steel frame, Mies added non-supportive bronze-tinted beams. Despite the austere aesthetic, the extravagant use of materials meant this was the world's most expensive building at the time. It served as a model for almost every NYC skyscraper that followed.

375 Park Avenue

Morgan Library & Museum

Since JP Morgan Jr donated his father's personal library to the people of New York in 1924, it has to be said that not many of the great unwashed have felt the need to venture in. The collection of Gutenberg Bibles, manuscripts and paintings has always given off enough of an elitist whiff to scare most people away. Renzo Piano's sublime 2006 expansion added an entrance on Madison Avenue, a glazed atrium and several galleries, increasing the exhibition space by more than 50 per cent – a design intended to beckon people in and pull together three existing buildings. It has made the Morgan a destination museum and host to many swanky, and lucrative, soirées. The old robber baron would have been pleased. *225 Madison Avenue, T 212 685 0008, www.themorgan.org*

Lincoln Center

To celebrate its 50th anniversary, in 2010, the city's pre-eminent performing arts venue undertook a $1.2bn renovation programme. The aim was to unify the 6.5-hectare complex, creating new spaces and revamping existing buildings, whose original architects included Eero Saarinen, Gordon Bunshaft and Philip Johnson. Diller Scofidio + Renfro and FXFOWLE were selected to tackle the overhaul of

Alice Tully Hall, which is part of the 1969 Julliard School designed by Pietro Belluschi and Eduardo Catalano. The performance facilities have been modernised and a glass-walled foyer has been added to the theatre; the school boasts a transparent, cantilevered canopy, which bursts out of the building towards Broadway.
70 Lincoln Center Plaza, T 212 875 5000, www.lincolncenter.org

Waterside Plaza

Perched on the edge of the East River, these four brutalist tower blocks, clad in red brick with streaks of black in spandrels, were designed by New York-based firm Davis, Brody & Associates (now Davis Brody Bond). Although the design was given the green light in 1963, construction did not begin until 1971, completing in 1974. The result is 1,470 apartments, many of which were intended to be subsidised housing. The central plaza within the complex is paved with large concrete slabs; in typical brutalist style the landscaping is probably best described as reserved. The only connection to mainland Manhattan is via a bridge at 25th Street over FDR Drive, making this effectively an island on an island.

30 Waterside Plaza off FDR Drive,
www.watersideplaza.com

New Museum

It isn't often that an art space has much in common with a trash can. In fact, SANAA's New Museum of Contemporary Art, launched in 2007, might be the only building to be clad in the same wire mesh as its home city's refuse receptacles. When the design – a series of piled-up silvery boxes – was revealed in 2003, it looked delightful yet impossible (not to mention improbable, given its location on the historically gritty Bowery). New York changes fast, though, and what once seemed so unlikely (a fine-art museum on a street known for its homeless shelters) now makes sense. It didn't hurt that a hip hotel, The Bowery (T 212 505 9100), opened up nearby. After your tour, visit the fun Bowery Diner (T 212 388 0052) next door. *235 Bowery, T 212 219 1222, www.newmuseum.org*

SHOPPING

THE BEST RETAIL THERAPY AND WHAT TO BUY

Retail therapy is as crucial as the Jungian variety in helping New Yorkers cope with love, life and the universe. For a one-stop shop, Barneys (660 Madison Avenue, T 212 826 8900), Saks (611 Fifth Avenue, T 212 753 4000) and Bergdorf Goodman (754 Fifth Avenue, T 212 753 7300) are hard to beat, while Henri Bendel (712 Fifth Avenue, T 212 247 1100) is a destination for beauty junkies.

For a more intimate shopping experience, head to downtown Manhattan and Brooklyn, to discover these areas' one-off shops. Odin (199 Lafayette Street, T 212 966 0026), with its smart mix of apparel and fragrances, is a hit with style-conscious gentlemen. Owen (see p084), a more recent fashion bellwether, stocks up-and-coming labels that are bound to become modern classics. To catch the wave of the urban-surf trend (or look like you know how), venture to Pilgrim Surf + Supply (68 N 3rd Street, T 718 218 7456) or Saturdays Surf (31 Crosby Street, T 212 966 7875). Design fans should explore Matter (opposite) and The Future Perfect (55 Great Jones Street, T 212 473 2500), which also has a branch (115 N 6th Street, T 718 599 6278) in Brooklyn. Two Soho stores to check out are Kiosk (see p077) for global curiosities, and BDDW (5 Crosby Street, T 212 625 1230), which sells handcrafted wooden furniture. In Tribeca, Espasso (38 N Moore Street, T 212 219 0017) is *the* showroom for Brazilian design, classic and contemporary.
For full addresses, see Resources.

Matter

Matter made its debut in Park Slope, Brooklyn, in 2003, opening a Soho branch in 2007. The design emporium continues to present a beautifully judged selection of furnishings and objects. International brands stocked include Established & Sons and Autoban. Among the local items, the delicate rings by Satomi Kawakita and metal coasters by Curios caught our eye. The in-house collection, MatterMade, is curated by the owner, Jamie Gray, who graduated from Pratt Institute with a degree in sculpture. Gray's eye is very much on craftsmanship when he seeks out makers, from woodworkers to glass-blowers. Recently featured were Bec Brittain's lighting, Meg Callahan's digitally printed quilts and tables by Andy Coolquitt. *405 Broome Street, T 212 343 2600, www.mattermatters.com*

Hollander & Lexer
H&L's second Brooklyn shop sells
trend-resistant and vintage items: a
sartorial mix that sealed the success of
the first Park Slope boutique. Peruse
the own-brand menswear and range of
accessories, such as Japanese scrubbing
brushes. Owners Yaz Benmira and Brian
Cousins designed the interior, which has
fabulous antique character.
103 Metropolitan Avenue, T 718 797 9117

Creatures of Comfort

Nolita has never lacked a good sprinkling of interesting retail outlets, but the launch of Creatures of Comfort in 2010 brought a new sense of vitality to this popular area. The shop presents an eclectic mix of products in a sprawling 215 sq m exposed-brick space, overseen by buyer and owner Jade Lai, who started the company in Los Angeles. Lai lures shoppers with goods spanning Japanese furniture to Bernhard Willhelm nail varnish. Best of all, though, is the fashion, mostly the womenswear, with the company's own ready-to-wear sitting alongside clothes by Slow and Steady Wins the Race, Isabel Marant and Henrik Vibskov, among others. There's also a project space in the shop, which hosts pop-ups, exhibitions and events. *205 Mulberry Street, T 212 925 1005, www.creaturesofcomfort.us*

Kiosk

Alisa Grifo's shop/gallery is so delightful because of its brilliant selection of everyday objects and its presentation concept: each product comes tagged with its history and provenance. Indeed, Grifo once worked as a curatorial assistant at the Cooper-Hewitt museum (see p032). In this treasure trove of a store, you'll find ongoing and one-off stock, from a Finnish Abloy padlock to a log carrier made from vegetable-tanned leather, a collaboration between US company Steele Canvas and Kiosk. The Bay Rum cologne (above), $20, hails from Massachusetts, and is made by Charles H Baldwin & Sons, which has been selling its wares (originally extracts and flavourings) since 1888. The subtle Bay Rum is made with oils of bay and clove. *2nd floor, 95 Spring Street, T 212 226 8601, www.kioskkiosk.com*

Partners & Spade

A studio-cum-store-cum-ideas-vault is probably the best way to describe this space run by Andy Spade, husband of accessories designer Kate, and veteran creative director Anthony Sperduti – aka Partners & Spade. The storefront of the Noho venue is used for art happenings and installations, and inside is an intriguingly random assemblage of products, from Best Made axes and a modern terrarium by garden designer Lindsey Taylor to a customised bike by Benedict Radcliffe. You may also come across art by the likes of Tobias Wong and JP Williams, a range of self-published found photography books and a few one-off fashion items. Partners & Spade is open at the weekend and by appointment during the week.
40 Great Jones Street, T 646 861 2827, www.partnersandspade.com

Billy Reid

Alabama-based William Reid had his first New York moment almost a decade ago, when his suits and casualwear won a quiet following among NYC's savvier dressers. He opened this store in 2008, selling his fine-woven blazers, chinos, corduroy jackets and Oxford shirts, plus a capsule collection of womenswear. Although it's in the heart of Gotham, the boutique displays Reid's Southern touch; there are vintage cabinets, a couch made from church pews, and a ceiling panelled with doors salvaged from a Mississippi schoolhouse. It's a civilised shop for the civilised shopper. A plaudit as Menswear Designer of the Year at the 2012 CFDA Awards means you will be seeing a lot more of Billy Reid's designs on dapper New York gents.
54 Bond Street, T 212 598 9355, www.billyreid.com

Malin+Goetz

Started in New York City in 2004, by Matthew Malin and Andrew Goetz, beauty super-brand Malin+Goetz opened its second boutique in 2009, in a former Dominican barbershop on the Upper West Side. Like the original branch in Chelsea (T 212 727 3777), this uptown store has the feel of a contemporary apothecary and boasts a unique interior. The Brooklyn-based architect Craig Konyk installed rich, walnut panels, salvaged from a Long Island mansion, which he juxtaposed with clinical white counters. Some original features, such as the tin ceiling, were maintained. The products smell gorgeous and are aimed at those with sensitive skin. M+G recently launched a store in Los Angeles (T 323 391 1884).
455 Amsterdam Avenue, T 212 799 1200, www.malinandgoetz.com

OHWOW

It may call itself a bookshop, but this tiny store in the West Village is about far more than reading material. Measuring just 18.5 sq m, it's the debut bricks-and-mortar outlet of the bicoastal OHWOW collective. Established in 2008 by Aaron Bondaroff and Al Moran, its aim is to facilitate exhibitions and one-off projects across various media, and publish art-themed books. The eye-popping space, designed by New York architect Rafael de Cárdenas, was partly inspired by the geometric prints found on traditional Navajo blankets. On the shelves are OHWOW's own books, esteemed style bibles and a selection of accessories. The collective also runs a gallery in Los Angeles (T 310 652 1711).
227 Waverly Place, T 646 370 5847, www.oh-wow.com/book-club

Baxter & Liebchen

Brooklyn-based Baxter & Liebchen is like a well-stocked modernist fleamarket. Selling 20th-century designs made up until the 1970s, the shop's collection is highly covetable, with a focus on Danish/Nordic designers. Sprawling across a 465 sq m warehouse in the Dumbo neighbourhood, B&L stocks up to 1,000 pieces at a time and regularly holds seasonal sales, when the discounts can be generous. Owner, Andrew Kevelson, has a penchant for the work of Arne Jacobsen and Hans Wegner, who, along with fellow midcentury masters such as Finn Juhl, are perennial bestsellers. Norwegian Arne Tidemand Ruud's lounge chair (above), was a standout piece for us. International shipping can be arranged.
*33 Jay Street, T 718 797 0630,
www.baxterliebchen.com*

Owen
Young retailer Phillip Salem is holding
his own in the saturated Meatpacking
District, with his first women's and
men's boutique, which opened in 2012
in a former gallery space. Yet it's Jeremy
Barbour's interior design – 25,000
brown paper sacks meticulously stapled
to the walls – that has grabbed the
attention of design and fashion nuts.
809 Washington Street, T 212 524 9770

Alexander Wang

A luxe but dishevelled aesthetic has made Alexander Wang's womenswear a smash with the fashion pack. Opened in 2011, on grungy-glam Grand Street, his Ryan Korban-designed flagship store is a mix of boutique, gallery and design den. The large, all-white space has high ceilings, marble floors and an oversized steel cage covered by seasonal installations. After browsing through Wang's sexy, downtown-friendly clothing and accessories, head to the centre of the shop, where a lounging area beckons you to kick off your heels or, considering the environs, your Converse. The leather sofa and brass table laden with reading material will ease any retail fatigue, as will the black mink hammock: simple but sumptuous, à la Wang.
103 Grand Street, T 212 977 9683,
www.alexanderwang.com

Modern Anthology

The two owners of this Dumbo furniture emporium, interior designers Becka Citron and John Marsala, worked on the *Man Caves* television series, which helped messy men clean up their homes. Their expertise is exercised in a design studio and this store. Modern Anthology takes a decidedly grown-up approach to interior design, with pieces that skew towards the masculine. The selections are made by Citron and Marsala, and their finely tuned instincts show an appreciation for the unexpected. Dotted throughout the store are vintage items, such as antique globes, barware and 100-year-old stag horns, as well as new furniture, accessories and a small range of clothing and grooming products.
*68 Jay Street, T 718 522 3020,
www.modernanthology.com*

SPORTS AND SPAS

WORK OUT, CHILL OUT OR JUST WATCH

From manicurists to masseurs, pedicurists to personal trainers, the Manhattanite has a small army of auxiliary support at his or her disposal, making this the ideal city for the beauty tourist. There are cool newcomers generating a worthy buzz, but let's not forget the tried and true: Cutler Salon (2nd floor, 47 W 57th Street, T 212 308 3838) makes dreams of runway hair a reality; New Yorkers still flock to Mario Badescu Spa (320 E 52nd Street, T 212 223 3728) for wallet-friendly facials; nobody in town does better nails than Haven Spa (150 Mercer Street, T 212 343 3515); and The Spa at Mandarin Oriental (80 Columbus Circle, T 212 805 8880) provides holistic treatments in a luxurious, sky-high setting.

Intense spinning is still popular (see p092), but also check out As One (www.as1effect.com) for high-intensity, small-group training. Continue the good work back home with skin care from local brand Malin+Goetz (see p081) and conceptual scents from CB I Hate Perfume (93 Wythe Avenue, T 718 384 6890).

There's a wide array of gyms throughout the city and most issue day passes. Otherwise, Central Park is the place to pound the pounds, or along the Hudson, where you can enjoy the breeze off the river. Catch the Knicks shooting hoops at Madison Square Garden (4 Pennsylvania Plaza, T 212 465 6741) and baseball at the Yankee Stadium in the Bronx (1 E 161st Street, T 718 293 6000). *For full addresses, see Resources.*

The Spa at Trump

Towering over Spring Street on Trump Soho's seventh floor, this spa combines old-world cleansing rituals with modern luxury. The standard is set by an entrance adorned with a fountain carved from Calacatta gold marble, a crystal and nickel woven-mesh chandelier, and a Macassar ebony doorway. But it's the hammam, New York's first, that takes top billing. Ivanka Trump hired architects DiGuiseppe to construct the spa. The hammam was hand-tiled with Turkish and Moroccan materials, and the domed ceiling has pinholes, echoing the classic design. For the *gommage*, attendants use *kese* mitts for exfoliation, and *torba* (cotton soap pouches) to work up a lather. Afterwards, mint tea awaits on a lush terrace.
246 Spring Street, T 212 842 5500, www.trumphotelcollection.com

Rudy's Barbershop
For their first East Coast branch, on the ground floor of the Ace Hotel (see p028), the owners of Rudy's (Wade Weigel, Alex Calderwood and David Petersen) wanted a salon with unisex appeal. Aiming for a utilitarian but quirky feel, they began the process with Brooklyn-based WRK Design, sourcing fixtures from a former Remington Ammunition factory in Connecticut. They also scoured New York for items such as the baked enamel wall panels and vintage lighting, both found on the Bowery. A long outdoor bench and tiny private garden were added, so you can socialise before and after your haircut. Post-appointment, visit the retail space upstairs, stocked with Kiehl's products, a book selection curated by art bookstore Karma (T 917 675 7508), and frozen goodies by People's Pops. *14 W 29th Street, T 212 532 7200, www.rudysbarbershop.com*

SoulCycle

Fragrant candles serve as a low-lit, non-competitive antidote to the high-octane atmosphere at SoulCycle, a spinning centre with an ever-expanding presence across the city. This flagship branch in Tribeca is a 575 sq m light-drenched space with three spin studios offering punishing workouts for the entire body. Along with conventional 45-minute spin sessions, SoulCycle has developed a diverse range of intense spinning classes, including the aptly named 60-minute Soul Survivor, and Soul Bands, a first-of-its-kind session which incorporates resistance bands hanging from the ceiling. Gym gear can be purchased from the SoulCycle Boutique, spin shoes are available to hire for $3 and towels are complimentary.

103 Warren Street, T 212 406 1300, www.soul-cycle.com

Takamichi Hair

Stepping into Takamichi Saeki's second-floor studio on the Bowery, it can be tricky to fathom what he's all about, which in this case is no bad thing. The gallerist-turned-hair-stylist enlisted friends and colleagues to convert the 186 sq m space into this striking salon, which could double as an art space. Belgian architect Sandra van Rolleghem pays tribute to 1960s Scandinavian style with streamlined white chairs and punchy red accents. Art by Santi Moix and Richard Hambleton graces the walls, and Belgian designer Éric Guen's origami chandeliers hang at the entrance. The owner's scissor skills are exemplary. His 'Takamichi Cut' is tailored to your head shape, texture and lifestyle. You'll leave feeling like the venue – one of a kind.
263 Bowery, T 212 420 7979,
www.takamichihair.com

Riverside Clay Tennis Courts

Riverside Park is one of the city's best green spaces next to the water. Running along the Upper West Side, it has a range of recreational facilities, including these 10 clay tennis courts, which are open from April until November. Turn-up-and-play passes can be purchased at the gate for $15, or go to The Arsenal in Central Park (T 212 360 8131, www.nycgovparks.org) to pick up a tennis permit, $200, which allows you unlimited play during the season. The courts are provided on a first come/first served basis and you'll need your own equipment. If the weather is inclement, Randall's Island, between East Harlem and Astoria, has a sports centre (T 212 427 6150) with indoor courts that can be hired by non-members, if they are reserved 48 hours in advance. *96th Street, T 212 978 0277, www.rcta.info*

ESCAPES

WHERE TO GO IF YOU WANT TO LEAVE TOWN

Gothamites claim that when you leave New York, you ain't going nowhere – although during the summer, the city's border seems to stretch to include the length of Long Island. When the going gets hot, the hot crowd gets going, to local beaches, including Jacob Riis, Fort Tilden and the Rockaways. If you can stand the humidity in town, your reward will be blissfully empty shops and restaurants. It's easy to escape the city at any time, in any direction, whether your taste is for an art tour (opposite), surfing off Montauk (see p102) or hiking in the Catskills. En route upstate, just an hour's drive from Manhattan, is the charming eight-room inn, Bedford Post (954 Old Post Road, Bedford, T 914 234 7800).

If you decide to go to the Hamptons, make sure you have a friend with a house, or have booked well in advance. Then pick up the Hampton Jitney (www.hamptonjitney.com), whose often glam passengers give new meaning to coach travel. It can be a bumper-to-bumper drive in summer traffic, so head to Shelter Island for a less intense getaway; take a ferry from North Haven or Greenport and stay at André Balazs' Sunset Beach hotel (35 Shore Road, T 631 749 2001). Closer to home, travel out on the B or Q trains to Brighton Beach and Coney Island. Rather than pack a towel, though, take a Russian phrase book; this enclave is known as Little Odessa, now more Moscow than Manhattan.
For full addresses, see Resources.

Dia:Beacon, Riggio Galleries

The Dia Art Foundation has supported artists since 1974. Its art collection is housed in an old Nabisco box factory in Beacon, remodelled by New York firm OpenOffice and artist Robert Irwin. The collection includes pieces by Walter De Maria, Michael Heizer and Richard Serra (*Torqued Ellipse II* and *Double Torqued Ellipse*, above). Rather than creating a Guggenheim-esque shell that risked overshadowing the art, the architects designed a loft-like space; in fact, this is where many artworks are created. Make it a day trip (it's an 80-minute train ride from Grand Central Station) and combine with a visit to the Richard B Fisher Center (T 845 758 7914), which is further up the valley. Closed Tuesdays and Wednesdays.
3 Beekman Street, Beacon,
T 845 440 0100, www.diabeacon.org

Noguchi Museum
Isamu Noguchi set up a studio and home
in Queens in 1960, which now form part
of this museum. Here you can view a
broad range of the artist's work, such
as his set designs for the dancer Martha
Graham. The tranquil garden, with some
of his sculptures, weeping cherry trees
and bamboo, is worth the trip alone.
9-01 33rd Road, Long Island City,
T 718 204 7088, www.noguchi.org

Glass House, New Canaan
The Connecticut town of New Canaan, about 40 miles north-east of NYC, boasts some of the finest examples of modern American architecture. The most famous is Philip Johnson's home, the Glass House (pictured), which he completed in 1949. It is perhaps the purest example of the International Style. Call in advance.
Visitor Center, 199 Elm Street, T 203 594 9884, www.philipjohnsonglasshouse.org

The Surf Lodge, Montauk

Surf's up at Montauk, a Long Island beach community beloved for its mellow vibe and pristine coastline. The Surf Lodge is a getaway for the city's suited and stressed. The chic-shack design of the 19 rooms (surf-inspired artwork, whitewashed walls, weathered-pine floors and eco products) was overseen by surfer and designer Alexandra Cassaniti. Explore Montauk's many natural highlights during the day, returning to the hotel come sunset for a sultry scene. Begin your evening at Byron, the in-house restaurant serving a market- and seafood-driven menu, then have cocktails at the bar, which has an outdoor terrace. If there are no rooms available here, book one at the equally buzzy Ruschmeyer's (T 631 668 2877). *183 Edgemere Street, T 631 668 1562, www.thesurflodge.com*

NOTES
SKETCHES AND MEMOS

RESOURCES

CITY GUIDE DIRECTORY

A

Acme 040
9 Great Jones Street
T 212 203 2121
www.acmenyc.com

Alexander Wang 086
103 Grand Street
T 212 977 9683
www.alexanderwang.com

The Americano 017
Hôtel Americano
518 W 27th Street
T 212 525 0000
www.hotel-americano.com

Ardesia 059
510 W 52nd Street
T 212 247 9191
www.ardesia-ny.com

The Arsenal 084
830 Fifth Avenue
T 212 360 8131
www.nycgovparks.org

As One 088
3rd floor
1841 Broadway
www.as1effect.com

AT&T Building 012
32 Sixth Avenue

Atera 040
77 Worth Street
T 212 226 1444
www.ateranyc.com

Austrian Cultural Forum 014
11 E 52nd Street
T 212 319 5300
www.acfny.org

B

Bar Boulud 047
1900 Broadway
T 212 595 0303
www.barboulud.com

Barneys 072
660 Madison Avenue
T 212 826 8900
www.barneys.com

Baxter & Liebchen 083
33 Jay Street
Brooklyn
T 718 797 0630
www.baxterliebchen.com

BDDW 072
5 Crosby Street
T 212 625 1230
www.bddw.com

The Beach 040
Dream Downtown
355 W 16th Street
T 212 229 2336
www.marblelane.com

Bemelmans Bar 060
The Carlyle
35 E 76th Street
T 212 744 1600
www.rosewoodhotels.com

Bergdorf Goodman 072
754 Fifth Avenue
T 212 753 7300
www.bergdorfgoodman.com

Le Bernardin 059
155 W 51st Street
T 212 554 1515
www.le-bernardin.com

Billy Reid 080
54 Bond Street
T 212 598 9355
www.billyreid.com

HOTELS

ADDRESSES AND ROOM RATES

Ace Hotel 028
Room rates:
double, $430;
Loft 811, $1,600
20 W 29th Street
T 212 679 2222
www.acehotel.com

Hôtel Americano 017
Room rates:
double, $450;
Uptown Studio, $680
518 W 27th Street
T 212 216 0000
www.hotel-americano.com

Andaz Wall Street 030
Room rates:
double, from $370;
Room 1513, from $410
75 Wall Street
T 212 590 1234
www.andaz.com

Bedford Post 097
Room rates:
double, from $395
954 Old Post Road
Bedford
T 914 234 7800
www.bedfordpostinn.com

The Bowery Hotel 071
Room rates:
double, from $325
335 Bowery
T 212 505 9100
www.boweryhotel.com

The Chatwal 021
Room rates:
double, from $795;
Producer Suite, from $4,690
130 W 44th Street
T 212 764 6200
www.thechatwalny.com

Crosby Street Hotel 022
Room rates:
double, from $605;
One Bedroom Suite, from $2,590
79 Crosby Street
T 212 226 6400
www.firmdale.com

Four Seasons 031
Room rates:
double, from $695;
Ty Warner Penthouse, $40,000
57 E 57th Street
T 212 758 5700
www.fourseasons.com/newyork

Gramercy Park Hotel 024
Room rates:
double, from $490
2 Lexington Avenue
T 212 920 3300
www.gramercyparkhotel.com

The James 027
Room rates:
double, from $525
27 Grand Street
T 212 465 2000
www.jameshotel.com

The Lowell 016
Room rates:
double, from $750
28 E 63rd Street
T 212 838 1400
www.lowellhotel.com

The Mercer 023
Room rates:
double, from $915
147 Mercer Street
T 212 966 6060
www.mercerhotel.com

The Nolitan 026
Room rates:
double, from $260
30 Kenmare Street
T 212 925 2555
www.nolitanhotel.com

The NoMad Hotel 020
Room rates:
double, from $440;
Grande Room, from $440;
Suite, from $745
1170 Broadway
T 212 796 1500
www.thenomadhotel.com

Ruschmeyer's 102
Room rates:
double, $205
161 Second House Road
Montauk
T 631 668 2877
www.kingandgrove.com

The Standard High Line 023
Room rates:
double, from $295
848 Washington Street
T 212 645 4646
www.standardhotels.com

Sunset Beach 097
Room rates:
double, from $345
35 Shore Road
Shelter Island
T 631 749 2001
www.sunsetbeachli.com

The Surf Lodge 102
Room rates:
double, from $625
183 Edgemere Street
Montauk
T 631 668 1562
www.thesurflodge.com

The Surrey 016
Room rates:
double, from $450
20 E 76th Street
T 212 288 3700
www.thesurrey.com

Thompson LES 016
Room rates:
double, from $300
190 Allen Street
T 212 460 5300
www.thompsonhotels.com

Wythe Hotel 018
Room rates:
double, from $335;
Manhattan View King Room, $400
80 Wythe Avenue
Brooklyn
T 718 460 8000
www.wythehotel.com

WALLPAPER* CITY GUIDES

Executive Editor
Rachael Moloney

Authors
Katie Chang
David Kaufman

Art Director
Loran Stosskopf
Art Editor
Eriko Shimazaki
Designer
Mayumi Hashimoto
Map Illustrator
Russell Bell

Photography Editor
Sophie Corben
Acting Photography Editor
Elisa Merlo
Photography Assistant
Nabil Butt

Chief Sub-Editor
Nick Mee
Sub-Editor
Emily Brooks

Editorial Assistant
Emma Harrison

Interns
Nathalie Akkaoui
Laura Font Sentis
Daniel Goldenberg

Wallpaper* Group Editor-in-Chief
Tony Chambers
Publishing Director
Gord Ray
Managing Editor
Jessica Diamond
Acting Managing Editor
Oliver Adamson

Contributor
Sara Henrichs

Wallpaper* ® is a registered trademark of IPC Media Limited

First published 2006
Revised and updated 2008, 2009, 2010, 2011 and 2013

© 2006, 2008, 2009, 2010, 2011 and 2013 IPC Media Limited

ISBN 978 0 7148 6457 0

All prices are correct at the time of going to press, but are subject to change.

Printed in China

PHAIDON

Phaidon Press Limited
Regent's Wharf
All Saints Street
London N1 9PA

Phaidon Press Inc
180 Varick Street
New York, NY 10014

Phaidon® is a registered trademark of Phaidon Press Limited

www.phaidon.com

A CIP Catalogue record for this book is available from the British Library.

PHOTOGRAPHERS

NEW YORK

A COLOUR-CODED GUIDE TO THE HOT 'HOODS

TRIBECA/THE BATTERY
Lower Manhattan embraces Wall Street and, to the north, hip stores and restaurants

UPPER WEST SIDE
This is Woody Allen territory, characterised by the apartment blocks of the bourgeoisie

WEST VILLAGE
This charming district has tree-lined streets, and plenty of chichi boutiques and eateries

SOHO
Fashion flagships draw the tourists, but there are interesting galleries and stores here too

UPPER EAST SIDE
Visit the swanky shops of Madison Avenue and some of the best museums in the world

MIDTOWN
The throbbing business heart of New York is also home to the neon-tastic Times Square

CHELSEA
New York's power art crowd gather day and night in this slick West Side neighbourhood

EAST VILLAGE/LOWER EAST SIDE
Super-cool bars, boutiques and galleries pepper this increasingly affluent part of town

For a full description of each neighbourhood, see the Introduction.
Featured venues are colour-coded, according to the district in which they are located.